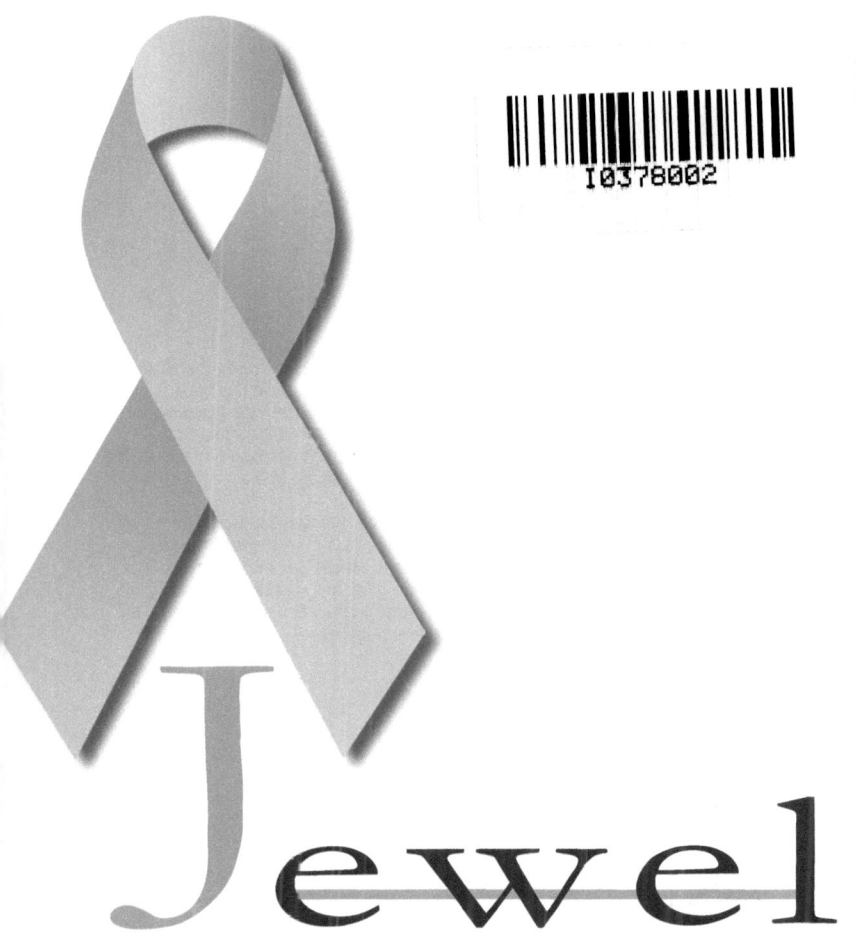

Jewel

The story of Julie's resilience
during her battle with cancer

DYLAN SMITH

First published by Busybird Publishing 2019

Copyright © 2019 Dylan Smith

ISBN
Print: 9781925949476
Ebook: 9781925949483

Dylan Smith has asserted his right under the Copyright, Designs and Patents Act 1988 to be identified as the author of this work. The information in this book is based on the author's experiences and opinions. The publisher specifically disclaims responsibility for any adverse consequences, which may result from use of the information contained herein. Permission to use information has been sought by the author. Any breaches will be rectified in further editions of the book.

All rights reserved. No part of this publication may be reproduced, stored in or introduced into a retrieval system, or transmitted in any form, or by any means (electronic, mechanical, photocopying, recording or otherwise) without the prior written permission of the author. Any person who does any unauthorised act in relation to this publication may be liable to criminal prosecution and civil claims for damages. Enquiries should be made through the publisher.

Cover design: Busybird Publishing

Layout and typesetting: Busybird Publishing

Busybird Publishing
2/118 Para Road
Montmorency, Victoria
Australia 3094
www.busybird.com.au

*'Don't cry or feel bad for me.
You only have one person to miss.
But me, I'm the one that will be
missing so many people.'*

Julie Smith, December 2018

Contents

Introduction	1
The 'C' Word	5
Remission	9
Comeback	13
Trifecta	15
Hope	19
Unsteady	23
Time & Existence	25
Surprise!	29
A Tickle in the Throat Becomes a Real Pain in the Neck	37
Sad Times at the El Royale	41
Run to You	45
Be in the Moment	47
A Rockstar with Angel Wings	51
Firsts	61
From One Mother to Another	65
Don't You Forget About Me	69

Introduction

Hi there, allow me to introduce myself. My name is Dylan Smith, and when I started to write this book I was 27 years old. The book that I am writing is a detailed journey of my mum's fight with cancer. Originally when I started writing this, it was a way for me to vent my anger, frustration and sadness, because holding it in and 'being tough' just wasn't working. But after giving my mum a rough copy to read as part of her Christmas present in 2018, and getting positive feedback from those who'd had a read, I decided to write something that not only showcases how strong and loved my mum was, but to hopefully inspire those still fighting this disease to not give up and to keep on fighting. But most of all, it's to show my mum's battle from a different perspective. So here we go!

Julie was born on 19 November 1964 to two loving parents, Ronald and Jacqueline. Growing up with her younger sister and three younger brothers, Mum always looked out for her younger siblings. And because of the nurture she showed as her siblings were growing up, Mum knew that parenthood was a path that would definitely call her name one day. Mum spent her adolescent years enjoying many of her first loves. Reading was one of those loves, but also sitting around the TV and enjoying her favourite TV shows. Some of the most notable of these TV shows were *Mork & Mindy*, *Countdown* and *The Restless Years*. But her all-time favourite pass-time was sitting around with my aunt on a Saturday, with a grilled cheese sandwich, watching *Hey Hey It's Saturday*.

Growing up, Mum absolutely loved Paul McCartney (but hated Linda McCartney) and listened to *Wings*, *The Police*, *ABBA* and, much later, Bryan Adams as well. She loved her music and every time she listened to her favourite bands or artists, she felt like she could escape for a little while. And while music was one of her escapes, travelling became her other escape.

Every year during her childhood, Mum and her family would travel to their home away from home, Bendigo – a place that held a significant piece of Mum, even in her final years.

Another place she would escape to was Blackwood. Every year, the family would go on a Christmas picnic with the social club, and on one of these picnics she met the love of her life, my dad, Ron Smith. The smartly dressed man, with the great moustache, that he was back then, quickly became captivated with Mum, as was she with him, and after years of dating they got engaged and eventually tied the knot on 20 May, 1989.

Although they were happy and content as a married couple, they really wanted to begin a family of their own. Two years later, parenthood came knocking and I was welcomed into the world, but not without a few stressful moments. I was born three months premature so I suppose you could say I was a headache to my parents as early as then. But my birth also came with a surprise for Mum as well. You see, upon having me Mum found out that she actually had two uteruses and only one kidney! But Mum, being who she was, took this as well as motherhood in her stride and besides this surprising news, began life as a mother.

A few years later, one child wasn't enough and they ended up with the 'perfect pair', as my sister was born three and a half years later. Growing up, my sister and I would always play the silliest pranks on each other. One of our favourite memories was when we were in primary school and it was a very hot summer's day. While we were playing under the sprinkler, I grabbed the hose tightly and caused it to kink. I asked my sister to look closely at the end of the hose to see if any water was coming out. As soon as she placed her head over the hose, I let go of the hose and the water rushed out and squirted her in the face. Mum and Dad weren't impressed, but they also couldn't help but laugh. As siblings, we were as close as can be growing up and still remain close to this day.

Childhood was often filled with its challenges. Tantrums, toilet training, and learning to tie shoe laces, but fast forward to 2010, and the challenges we had previously faced, would be nothing in comparison to what would happen next.

The 'C' Word

The 'C' word.

No, it's not Christmas, although it could be described by another word starting with C. I guess for now you could call it 'See You Next Tuesday' (kids, don't ask your parents, and parents, don't elaborate). No, I'm talking about cancer, but I do prefer that other name. I cannot begin to understand what people diagnosed with cancer in any form are going through: experiencing it yourself must be worse than anything I have experienced as an outsider. This story focuses on a couple of forms of cancer, and this is where our story truly begins.

I was 18 going on 19, fresh out of high school and ready to attack the big wide world with hope and hopelessness wrapped into one. You hear stories of people who are struck down with some form of cancer. You can't imagine what they and their families are going through. But sadly, we would find out soon enough.

While showering one day, Mum noticed a lump behind her left breast. Being the ever-cautious woman that she was, she went to have some scans done. That was when we were introduced to breast cancer.

Fuck. What does this mean? Where do we go from here? And why the fuck does cancer exist? Why is it always the good people who have to be struck down?

All of these questions and expletives ran through my mind, and to this day the questions remain (with even more expletives thrown in for good measure). And speaking of good measure, it was at this time that Dad was dealing with prostate cancer as well. Double fuck, am I right?! The twin rocks of our family struck down at once, how lucky were we? Someone buy us a lottery ticket! But thankfully, after having parts of his prostate removed, Dad recovered well and has since continued living his life with no additional side effects.

Proving what we already knew, of how much of a rock Mum was, she made the decision to undergo a radical mastectomy operation. Then, some weeks after her operation, Mum began her dance with chemotherapy. It was fair to say that the chemo didn't feel like easing her into the dance gently – instead, it just knocked her about immensely! After the first few sessions Mum seemed to be picking up the dance routine quickly, but then out of nowhere chemo would up the ante and Mum was hit for six. At this point in time, you could say that cancer and chemotherapy shared the same nickname starting with 'C' ...

Days of bed rest and chuck buckets followed, but as soon as we thought we had mastered the dance of chemotherapy, it reared its ugly head again and we went toe-to-toe for another battle.

But finally, after many sessions of chemotherapy, it was finished! And we all celebrated with an alcoholic beverage (kids wait until you're 18!). That became somewhat of a tradition as we ticked off each stage of her remission.

Now, for someone who prided herself on being presentable when going out or having people over to visit, seeing her hair falling out while combing it was hard. But like the fighter she was, she took it all in her stride with a smile on her face and began wearing head scarves (and beanies for when the weather wasn't kind). At this point in time, Mum began to realise how much support she had while fighting this beast. A close family friend of ours, who also happened to be Mum's best friend Ellen, shaved her head in support of Mum losing her hair. Mum's job during this time was working in the canteen of my old primary school. And while the kids were completely respectful in realising Mum had lost her hair, there were the small group of kids who didn't understand why she was wearing beanies or bandanas. Thankfully, with Ellen's help, Mum was able to get past the weird looks and constant questions from the students.

But even with all of that going on, Mum hid her tears from us, thinking we didn't know she was struggling. She smiled when we needed it and hugged us because she needed it. But as we were only at the infancy stage of our brush with cancer, Mum began to look forward to her next destination: the five-year remission goal!

Remission

Remission. *Noun. From the Latin remittere (send back, restore). Remission is described as a temporary or permanent decrease or subsidence of manifestations of a disease.*

– Marriam-Webster Dictionary, Dictionary.com

Key word there, *temporary*. But I'll get to that soon.

Year by year, we got back to living our lives, and bit by bit, we started to forget about cancer. It got to a point where the cancer felt like that family member that shows up, uninvited, to family events. You hate that you let them into your home, but you're fucking thankful when they leave. And after a while, you stop thinking about them altogether. You know they were around, but they aren't a part of your lives anymore. Well, at least that's what we thought.

You've heard of the seven-year itch, right? You know, when apparently happiness declines after year seven of a marriage? Well, for us, we experienced the five-year itch, and we were joined together in holy matrimony with cancer, the itch we couldn't scratch.

Cancer, much like Pokémon, can evolve into many forms. For us, its primary form was breast cancer and its secondary form was breast cancer that had hopped on a bus from its first destination and moved up to the neck. I didn't know too much about cancer before all of this, but I definitely did not know that secondary breast cancer was a thing. But it had missed our company, and we had a family reunion with that family member who likes to show up uninvited.

Mum was three years cancer-free at this stage, and at the time of this new diagnosis Mum's mum, my grandmother, was undergoing major heart surgery. But Mum, forever the one to think of others instead of herself, decided to hold off on the news that we had been invited to another party, and that the guest of honour wasn't taking no for an answer.

Now for those who are interested in history, in 1939 the movie *Wizard of Oz* was released, and as a child it was one of my mum's favourite movies. The film was filled with many unforgettable quotes, but one that really sticks out and is poignant with this story is 'there's no place like home'.

They also say home is where the heart is, or home is where you make it. But for us, home became the hospital. There were more tests, another biopsy and another arduous wait on results, but sure enough we had been met with cancer yet again.

Because of the positioning of this latest critter, Mum couldn't speak without sounding croaky or like she smoked ten packets of cigarettes a day. We didn't know it at the time, but the only way we would be able to hear Mum's 'original' voice was through her voicemail message on her phone, and it wasn't something we realised we would miss, until we did.

But nevertheless, this was the mark that cancer was leaving to show that it had come and gone, just like that, in the blink of an eye. And with what felt like TV repeats of *Frasier* or *Two and a Half Men*, we were then turning on the TV to watch a familiar show. *Remission 2.0.*

It began to feel smoother the second time around though. We knew what was expected, and we knew how many years we were working toward.

But just as we did after the first time we began living our lives again, we celebrated milestone birthdays, births in the family and eventually got on with living our lives. So much so we got to the point where we were absolutely happy again. We lived in everyone's successes and loved that little bit more in the tough times, but overall, cancer felt like a thing of the past, and we began planning our future as a family.

Full steam ahead!

Comeback

Comeback. *A comeback can be described in many different ways, but one that works for our scenario is to stage a 'return ... after a period away'.*

– Collins Dictionary

Comebacks happen all the time. Most notably, you would say John Farnham is well known for a comeback and, most recently, the TV show Roseanne has done it (one of those was more successful than the other, but I'll leave that up to you to decide). All I'm saying is comebacks, whether warranted or not, can become a thing of beauty, or they can turn your world upside down.

For Mum, she took her comeback in her stride, but she was living life to the fullest! She returned to work as a canteen attendant, and then later as a teacher's aide, she attended school council meetings, dropped off and picked up my dad from work, right up until his retirement in December 2016.

But as much as Mum was trying to move on and live life to the fullest, something had grabbed hold of Mum, and it wasn't letting her go. No matter how many rounds we went against it, it lingered. It lingered like a fart on a long road trip, and you can't open the car windows to release the stench. It's fair to say this next battle left a shit taste in everyone's mouths.

This, my friends, is what I like to call the trifecta, and if I was a betting man, I know who my money would be on!

Trifecta

A trifecta is described as a run of three wins or grand events.

– **Oxford Dictionary**

If you've been following me since the beginning, you will notice we haven't had many wins or grand events. But something was different this time. This time, I couldn't see a light at the end of the tunnel. The doctors and nurses (although we cannot fault a single thing they have done and continue to do) were at a loss as to what could be done.

Alright. Let me set the scene.

It was mid-2017. We were living our normal lives filled with meetings, conference calls, traffic, date nights, football training and matches and not getting enough sleep (but refusing to go to bed earlier). Anyway, I digress. During the months of May and June, Mum was struck down with a severe case of vertigo. Her only solace was lying down in bed. She had all the signs you would expect of vertigo. The nausea, vomiting, jerking eye movements, they were all evident. And while her job was put on hold to deal with this vertigo, her smile and positive outlook shone through like a ray of sunshine on a cloudy Melbourne winter day.

So now I ask you a question. As a parent, what could be the worst phone call a mother or father could receive regarding their children? I can only assume that a phone call from the police with terrible news involving an accident would be fairly high on the list. But what call could a 27-year-old son receive that would make his heart sink just as much? Well since you asked nicely, I will tell you.

It was the Queen's Birthday weekend, and I was away for the weekend. I was having trouble with my phone, so trying to charge it was about as useful as a white crayon. But somehow I managed to wake up to a semi-charged mobile phone the next day, and thought I'd better catch up on all of the morning's news headlines. And of course, by news headlines I mean catch up on everything I'd missed on Facebook, Instagram and Snapchat from the night before. But when you see a missed call and a voicemail message from your mum, you think of one of two things. One: I'd forgotten something important at home for my weekend away and Mum realised I'd left it and would need it this weekend. Or two: Mum's wishing you all the best for your weekend, and will see you when you return, but can you also grab some bread or milk on the way home? But I received neither of those normal sounding messages and looking back, I absolutely wish I had received those messages.

No, our terrific run of luck had continued and I was left with a voicemail message saying that Mum was in hospital and that when I could, could I call her back? Now, I've never been the type of person to say that there was something or someone watching over me, or our family for that matter, but for that brief moment I feel like someone wanted me to have enough juice in my phone to be able to listen to that message so that I could call her back.

Now, hands up those who have been on a rollercoaster, or turned a corner too quickly while driving, which results in your stomach rising up until it now resides in your throat? That's how I felt after returning the call. I was told that she was in the hospital and that the vertigo she was experiencing wasn't actually vertigo at all. Scan results the previous day had shown that she had multiple tumours toward the base of her brain, where the head connects to the spine.

Fuck. Fuck. Fuck.

Next were the tears and for a split second, I actually felt like my soul had left my body and I was just a shell of a man, kneeling there hopelessly with no life in him whatsoever and crying uncontrollably. The doctors weren't sure whether or not these tumours were cancerous but had decided that Mum would have emergency surgery the next morning to remove what they could of the little 'See You Next Tuesdays'.

Now Mum, again forever thinking of others before thinking of herself, instructed me to stay the final night of my weekend away, and to visit the hospital on my way home after her operation. So what does this 27-year-old son do when his mum tells him to do something? He goddamned listens to his mother, that's what!

While the weekend away was definitely something my partner and I needed – our lives were so busy that we mainly saw each other on weekends – the final night was definitely overshadowed by what my mum would be going through the next morning. And all my partner and I could do was spend the final night of our weekend away together and hope. Hope everything goes well. Hope for a great outcome and for our luck to change, because at that moment it felt like we were on our final dollar, and we had a poor hand against the dealer.

Hope

Hope. A feeling of expectation and desire for a particular thing to happen.

– **Oxford Dictionary**

Now, as a kid, every year at Christmas time I would always hope that I had been a good boy for long enough throughout the year that I would get some, if not all, of the presents on my Christmas wish list. But as I got older, and in particular in this very moment, I hoped that the news I had received the day before was all a dream and that when I woke up the next morning, I would be returning home to a smiling Mum greeting us from the kitchen and asking why I had forgotten the aforementioned bread or milk. But no, reality had taken control of the steering wheel now and I was heading to the hospital to visit Mum after her eight-hour long operation.

A battered and bruised woman lay in front of me as I made my way into the room. She was still the mum I knew, but her words spoke of her worry about what lay ahead. She knew something was not right. And after weeks of recovery, we got the dreaded news that the tumours found in the base of her skull were, in fact, cancerous.

Yeah, that little fucker had returned once again and this time, he had some friends with him.

I say 'had' some friends with him because the doctors were able to remove one of them. The one they couldn't completely remove had to stay there. The doctors said if they had tried to get it all, it would have left Mum a vegetable.

They decided after a further few weeks of recovery that they would begin radiation. Hello again, cancer, you big bully. Are you ready for another round?!

Again, our ever well-presented Mum would experience hair loss, nausea, the occasional bruising and skin burns and other associated symptoms, but they were confident that the little bastard they left there would shrink in size and therefore allow Mum to get back to a healthier lifestyle. And things were looking great for a while too, but then Mum began to show signs that this fight wasn't over just yet. The tumour was on the ropes, but he was hanging in there, throwing a few left-right combinations to give himself some breathing space, before meticulously planning out his comeback to take the fight on a points decision. But if winning was his ultimate goal, then I feel like he could see the finish line while we were stuck competing in a race with concrete-filled shoes.

Unsteady

Unsteady. Liable to fall or shake. Not steady in position.

– **Oxford Dictionary**

That was how we knew something wasn't right. Mum was still unsteady on her feet, often bumping into walls and knocking into things like she was nine or ten Bacardi-and-cokes deep. But no, she was stone cold sober, but you wouldn't have guessed that. She was unsteady, felt like there was someone with their hands around her head, slowly tightening their grip. Yep, we were right, this time did feel different. Although you wouldn't have known it felt different to Mum, she just took it all in her stride. And if you asked her how her day was after getting home from work, she would always say 'good', even if it wasn't.

It was now that Mum would begin to have regular scans and consultations with her GP, and her current job as a teacher's aide at the same primary school she worked at in the canteen was put on hold.

I was always told that Mum would cry and break down, but if she ever did, my sister and I never saw it. She was very good at that, but also very open and honest and would always answer any questions that we had, no matter how tough it may have been.

But although she would always answer our questions to the best of her ability, there was one question that began to cross our minds, one that we never thought we would have to ask, and one that I couldn't bring myself to ask. That question was, *'How long do you have left?'*

Time & Existence

Time. *The indefinite continued progress of existence and events in the past, present and future regarded as a whole.*

– Oxford Dictionary

After this most recent diagnosis, time became more about the continued progress of existence in which we could create memories with Mum. So many questions raced through my mind when asking Mum if the doctors could say how long she had left. And their honest and heartbreaking answer was, 'We're not sure'. Besides receiving that voicemail message, hearing this was another kick in the guts. But after sitting back and really thinking about the situation, I daresay they had other reasons for not being sure of Mum's lifespan. Were they hoping that the radiation would take effect and, slowly but surely, Mum would regain all of the little bits about her that makes anyone she met instantly happy to be in her presence? Who knows. Or would she cease to exist and become a shell of who she once was?

Existence. *Described as the fact or state of living or having objective reality, [or, a definition that really resonated with me and this particular story] continued survival.*

– Oxford Dictionary

How long does one survive on this planet for? Is there a timer that hangs over your head that gradually counts down while you go about your life, until one day the years, months, days, hours, minutes and seconds all just reach zero? Do we have a fixed amount of years that we are alive for or is it unknown to us that our existence will prematurely come to an end?

Well, with not knowing how much longer Mum had, we began to take life by the balls and make the most of any opportunity. In November 2018, Mum was heading towards her 54th birthday, and with everything that had happened, Mum decided she wasn't going to celebrate it that year. She was too tired, but also content with not celebrating her birthday that year. But after speaking with my sister, we decided that Mum *would*, in fact, celebrate her birthday.

We would throw Mum a surprise birthday party instead.

Now, as Mum's health began to deteriorate further, she couldn't leave the house without the newest season fashion accessory. For others it may be the newest earrings, a necklace or even the freshest smelling perfume or aftershave. No, as if cancer hadn't had enough laughs, Mum's newest accessory was a wheelchair. Trying to get Mum out of the house just became fucking harder now that there was a wheelchair to contend with.

But so far, with any real setback that we had come across, we had always managed to find a solution to any problem. And as the old saying goes, 'Where there's a will, there's a way!'

Surprise!

As Mum was a big fan of shopping, we planned to have her leave the house for a couple of hours on the day of her actual birthday, November 19th, to visit a new Coles that had opened up nearby, with coffee and cake to follow that at the nearby cafe. We had planned for all of our close family and friends to bring along a plate of savoury foods and some desserts so we didn't have to worry about a massive clean up after the party. It was certainly going to be a surprise to surpass all previous surprises. But little did we know that soon enough, the surprise was on all of us.

The day before her surprise 54th birthday party, Mum returned from the local shopping centre with severe pains in her kidneys, and unfortunately she was passing blood as well. Later that afternoon, Mum was taken to the emergency department of our local hospital. Our hope for the surprise party the next day was remaining high. We created a group chat with all of our family members, to keep them updated on Mum and the party's progress. But it appeared that Mum's original wish to not celebrate her birthday would come to fruition, because if cancer was a 'See You Next Tuesday', then what would come next could only be described as a fucking party pooper.

Surprise! It's fucking kidney stones. As if breast cancer, cancer in Mum's neck and cancer in the brain weren't enough. It had to be kidney stones ...

Well, in what was anti-poetic justice, Mum celebrated her 54th birthday in hospital recovering from having one of her kidney stones removed and having a mesh inserted to keep the other one in check. Mum was released from hospital a few days later, but would return a couple of weeks later to have the other kidney stone removed. But now that Mum was home and relaxing as best she could, it was time to put our plans in motion for Surprise Party 2.0.

So, on November 25th we managed to get Mum out of the house for a couple of hours to get everything sorted. I ran out to grab the cake while my sister and Dad were left to set up the backyard. Not long after the backyard began to take shape, our guests started arriving and everything was ready to go. Now all we were waiting on was Mum.

Mum and I had the Bon Jovi concert at the MCG the following weekend, so we organised with Mum's friend

Surprise!

Ellen that I would meet them at the car and wheel Mum in the wheelchair around the side of the house to the backyard – to practice for the following weekend. As I grabbed Mum from the car, my heart began to race and my mouth began to dry out, but Mum never suspected a thing. Wheeling Mum around the side of the house to the backyard and having 30–40 family and friends yelling *'surprise'* is not something Mum, nor anyone who attended, will ever forget. What followed was an afternoon full of tears, laughter and so much love. The videos of that day and Mum's tearful, heartfelt speech still bring tears to my eyes to this day.

Since Mum's most recent diagnosis, we were focused on creating as many memories as possible. What Mum didn't realise is she showed us how important it was to live in the moment, because before we knew it, a moment would soon become a memory.

A young, fresh faced Julie.

Ron & Julie, love at first sight.

Julie on her Wedding Day.

Julie & Ron - their ride awaits.

Julie (dressed as Dorothy) for Book Week.

Julie (Dorothy), Ron (the Scarecrow) for Laura's 21st Birthday.

The Smith's at Julie's 50th Birthday.

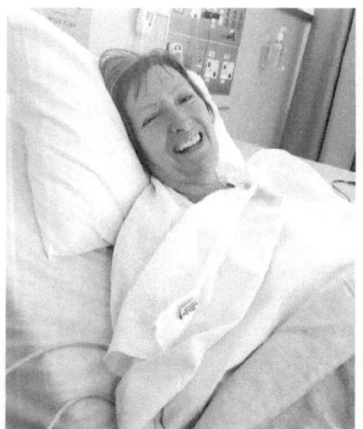
Even Hospitals couldn't silence her trademark smile.

Love, always.

Julie looking posh at high tea.

Julie & Rosie.

Julie & Emily, at Julie's surprise 54th birthday, November 2018.

Julie & Dylan at the Bon Jovi concert December, 2018.

Christmas 2018, our last Christmas together.

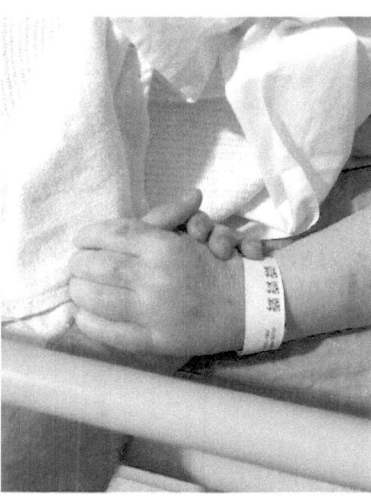

One last hand hold, before Julie gained her wings.

A Tickle in the Throat Becomes a Real Pain in the Neck

More memories were made following on from Mum's surprise birthday party.

A week following Surprise Party 2.0, Mum, my aunty and I went to Bon Jovi's Melbourne concert. Originally, I had purchased seated tickets, but due to Mum's rapid decline I had prayed that I was able to organise for those tickets to be changed to allow wheelchair access. Thankfully my prayers were answered, so Mum was able to enjoy the concert in the comfort of her wheelchair.

It was around this time as well that Dad had installed railings in the toilet and shower so that it was easier for Mum to complete daily tasks that others may find simple and easy, but for her were a real workout.

Just like that, in the blink of an eye, Christmas was here and gone. Mum managed to push herself out of the couch and the wheelchair and into my car to share Christmas lunch at my aunt and uncle's house. I will never forget the smile on Mum's face as we took a family photo together, my dad and sister included. A photo that we will treasure forever.

2019 rolled around quickly, and while Mum and Dad would usually be off to a New Year's getaway for a couple of weeks, this year it was more TV shows and relaxing at home, as opposed to TV shows and relaxing, but with a pool nearby. But even though she wasn't on a holiday, Mum was still able to enjoy herself from the comfort of her own home.

Mum, despite finding things very difficult at this stage, willed herself out of the house to attend her mum's 80th birthday lunch. As hard as it was for her to get up out of bed and off the couch, she did it, she was there and it was a great afternoon for all of us.

It was not long after this that Mum began to develop a cough that sounded like she smoked a pack a day, right around the same time her health deteriorated further. Mum would now rely on Dad to get her to the toilet, to the shower and to bed, and I would help her where I could. After a few weeks, her cough began to subside and we could finally continue to make memories to last a lifetime.

Over the New Year period, we had all of our old family video tapes converted into DVDs, and we spent countless weeknights and weekends glued to the TV reminiscing about our lives. Life was really fucking good!

But as soon as we enjoyed the good times and we felt like we were 'swimming freely', life managed to grab the fishing rod and reel us back in.

Mum's chest cold had reared its ugly head once again. After home visits from the nurses, Mum was given various cough medicines, but nothing seemed to break down the build-up of phlegm and other nasties (sorry for the mental image). It got to a point while I was at work, that Mum had asked for an ambulance to be called as she had trouble catching her breath after constantly coughing.

It was probably after 6–8 weeks of the cold hanging around that we began to think that maybe something wasn't right, but after all, if the nurses weren't worried, then we would keep the faith as well (a Bon Jovi reference for all of you playing along at home).

But as we would eventually find out, Mum knew her body all too well and as much as the nurses weren't worried about it, Mum knew something wasn't right. She knew something wasn't right way back in 2010, and here we were in 2019: she still knew something wasn't right, and it would take a while for us to catch up to what she already knew.

Sad Times at the El Royale

Mum's cough gradually began to sound nastier and she would, more often than not, struggle to catch her breath. As it had become increasingly worse after I put Mum to bed and I went to bed, I would always put my ceiling fan on – not because it was hot, but more so because I needed some sort of noise to block out the sounds of her coughing, or struggling to catch her breath. Without it, I wouldn't sleep much, and I found that I would become very anxious.

Over time, that would just become the norm. Mum would be put in bed, she would watch TV, and I would get ready for bed and make sure the ceiling fan was on. As hard as I thought it was at the time, it couldn't prepare me for what would come.

I remember this as clear as day, because it was the night before round one for our local footy season.

I think I had managed a nap of about an hour or so before Dad came rushing in at 1:30 in the morning on April 6th. Mum wanted an ambulance to be called, as she was struggling to breathe again, but this time, she was really worked up. As annoyed as I was at the time for being woken up with a game of footy the next day, it soon melted away after seeing the look of terror on Mum's face.

Five minutes passed after calling 000 before the ambulance arrived, and the paramedics began to check on Mum. We informed them of Mum's current situation with her health and her inability to walk without support. While examining her, the paramedic asked Mum 'Is there anything else you need?' and without delay Mum replied 'a cure'. We all just sat there in silence, until after what felt like an hour, the paramedic replied, 'you're beautiful'.

After examining Mum and getting her breathing issues seemingly under control, the ambos agreed that sending her to the hospital for further tests would be the best course of action. As Dad rode along in the ambulance with her, I began to pack a bag of things for Mum to meet them at the hospital shortly after.

After some X-rays, Mum was told that they couldn't see anything on her chest but wanted to keep her over the weekend to run some more tests, they planned on having her home early the following week.

Sleep deprived and anxious, Dad and I returned home later that morning around five, to try and get whatever sleep we could before round one of footy and now adding visiting Mum in hospital later that day to the list. But before we could even think of any of that, it was finally time for one thing. Sleep.

Round one had come and gone, we started the season with a 70-point win, but as mentally exhausted as I was during the game, it all faded away once we visited Mum in hospital. Tired but comfortable, Mum was back to her normal, effervescent self. No care in the world for her needs, only making sure that we were all doing alright.

Mum had informed us that they planned on giving her a CT scan to get further information the following day. They were confident it would give them some answers to Mum's heavy breathing and shortness of breath. Little did we know that soon, we would all have the answers none of us wanted!

We had been home for only an hour or two after visiting Mum when we received a phone call from the hospital. Now, at this stage, Dad and I had sat down to watch *Bad Times at the El Royale*, and if anyone can actually tell me what happens in that movie I would be very grateful, because from the moment Dad hung up the phone I was numb to the rest of the movie and to everything else around me.

One of the doctors who had just received Mum's CT scan results was on the phone. And again, Mum knew her body to a T. We were told that Mum had tumours and clots on her lungs and she was really only getting the use of one lung, hence the shortness of breath. Dad hung up the phone and came in to tell me the news. He also mentioned that the doctors had said they had given Mum all of a couple of weeks left to live. Dad and I sat there staring at nothing, movie playing in the background.

The tears came first. Anger was next, as we looked at each other and said it wasn't fucking fair. But while we were home dealing with the news ourselves, Mum was in hospital hearing the news from the doctors as well. And what breaks my heart the most is knowing that we couldn't be there with her at the time she found out.

Difficult phone calls were made to our family members that night. I can't even remember what I said now, but one thing that was for certain was that I desperately wanted to get to the hospital to see Mum. And that would happen the following morning.

Run to You

I don't think I slept much at all that night. And there wasn't much dialogue between Dad, my sister and me the following morning. We kept looking at the clock waiting for visiting hours to open. Little did we know, until a few visits later, that we could have visited earlier if we wanted to (being immediate family) and if Mum had her way, she would have had us there with her from eight every morning.

Walking into Mum's hospital room for the first time after hearing the news was probably the most nerve-wracking thing I think I've experienced. I felt sick and really anxious, but all of that soon went away when I saw Mum's face. As soon as Dad entered the room, he and Mum burst into tears as they emotionally embraced.

After eventually calming down and pushing through the tears, we just sat there quietly looking at Mum as she slept while she received her medication. Again, true to the person she is, after waking up the first thing she asked was how we were all doing with the news. 'Fucking shit' I think was my response. But Mum, trying to remain calm but failing to do so, said through tears 'I'm not afraid to die, I'm afraid of missing you all. I have no regrets in my life. I have two beautiful children who are happy and healthy, with beautiful supportive partners. I have a husband and family who I love dearly'.

Talk about an emotional rollercoaster. I held myself together for most of that day, but with every new visitor, I just sat there crying as they all embraced Mum, their first visit since hearing the news.

So, after visiting hours had finished for the day, tired and emotional, we left Mum for the night before preparing ourselves to do it all over again the following day. 'Goodbye Mum, I love you,' I said as I left the room, to which she replied, 'I love you more, to the moon and back.'

Be in the Moment

Throughout my life, my mum has taught me many lessons. From socks being more preferable on my feet before my shoes, to looking left and right before crossing a road, to washing more than a couple times a week (younger me, not me now) and many more life lessons.

But without her knowing it, and if she did, she didn't let on, Mum taught me another important lesson: be in the moment. With the way our lives are at the moment in terms of technology, I had forgotten that sometimes it's best to put the phone away. Emails can wait, Facebook can definitely wait. Before Mum was admitted to hospital, I would often just sit next to her while she watched TV, or lay next to her while she was watching TV in bed, and just talk to her about anything, or even just look over at her from time to time. But for the time that Mum was in hospital (besides the occasional phone call or text message checking in on how Mum was) I would find myself looking over to her again while she was resting. I would wonder what she was dreaming about. And when she was awake, when she seemed to stare off into the distance, I would wonder what she was thinking.

Was she beginning to see a light ahead or shiny golden gates with a padlock on them? Entwined on the gate, was there a timer counting down the months, days, hours, minutes or even seconds to when it would be unlocked for her to enter? I couldn't be sure. But she definitely did teach me the value of a moment.

After a few days of being in one of the wards in the hospital, Mum had gotten her wish to be moved into palliative care. I had heard of palliative care before, and I might have experienced it with my Pa when I was very young, but to see all of the patients whose rooms surrounded Mum had made me question how we got here in what felt like no time at all. Mum was fighting this bastard for almost nine years to this point, but it feel like just yesterday when she went in for her first lot of scans, and now we were in the last place she would be before she went 'home'.

While in palliative care we tried to make Mum as comfortable as possible and do our best to grant any wish or do anything that she wanted. For the first four days of being in palliative care, she really wanted us to bring our dog, Rosie, for a visit. Rosie hadn't seen Mum since she was whisked away in an ambulance almost a week earlier. Rosie knew something was up, because every night we would come home, walk in the door and say hello, but then she would run to the window and wait. We knew she was waiting for Mum, but how can you tell your pet she might not be coming home when you cannot fully comprehend it yourself?

But finally, a week before Good Friday, we brought Rosie in to see Mum. My gut feeling was 'this was it': we would bring Rosie in, she and Mum would have a cuddle, Mum would say her goodbyes, we would take Rosie home and then we would get a call the next morning to say that Mum had held on until Rosie's visit, but she's now in a better place. But thankfully, Mum and Rosie had shared their cuddles, Mum had shed her tears (as we all did) and we came in the next morning to her smiling face watching the TV.

The week before the Easter break was a busy one. I am thankful and grateful that my employer let me work half days, which meant I could work in the morning and then head straight to the hospital in the afternoon to visit Mum.

Good Friday rolled around and I came into the hospital with my partner to find Mum wasn't in her room. As my heart began to race and I started to panic, I saw my sister in the courtyard. As I edged closer to the courtyard, I could see that the nurses had wheeled Mum out to the courtyard to enjoy the surprisingly warm April day that we were experiencing. Mum's smile reigned supreme that day. For once, she seemed to enjoy her time in the hospital.

Easter arrived a couple of days later, and to say it wasn't an ideal one would be a fair statement. The day itself was good, we were surrounded by loved ones. But if I were to compare it to every Easter I had experienced in my 27 years, this one was definitely not in my top 10 memories. Every Easter for as long as I could remember, Mum would sneak out the night before – rain, hail or shine – to hide Easter eggs around the yard for the Easter Egg hunt the following morning. She kept this going right up until 2018. I wasn't involved in the last few hunts and, looking back now, it's memories, like those that will make me laugh and cry at the same time.

A Rockstar with Angel Wings

Easter Monday was here. Usually, my day is filled with relaxing, mentally preparing myself for a shorter working week (which is often more stressful than a normal working week) and Geelong v Hawthorn at the MCG. Well this year, the only thing that was normal compared to other Easter Mondays was that Geelong and Hawthorn were playing at the MCG.

It was right around the time that the game started that Mum's health began to deteriorate. It was nothing major, but the doctors were keeping a close eye on her. I remember this day clearly because my cousin wanted to visit Mum as he couldn't see her over Easter. He had planned to visit her this coming Wednesday. Unfortunately, I had to message him to tell him that Mum was slowly going downhill and if he wanted to visit, sooner rather than later would be ideal.

We left the hospital that night, nervous but hopeful. I had planned to get up extra early the following morning, make the family breakfast and take Dad to the hospital earlier than normal to spend the day with Mum. And little did we know, time was of the essence.

As planned, we all got up really early the following day, and while rubbing the sleep from my eyes, I began to cook eggs and bacon for the rest of the weary household. I think that day we ate because we had to, but we definitely didn't take our time to enjoy the meal, for not long after taking the final bite, Dad and I were in the car to the hospital while my sister and her partner were following shortly behind.

After finding a parking spot close by and making our way into the palliative care ward, we arrived to find Mum dozing in and out of sleep before keeping her eyes open just long enough to register that we had arrived. After a quick little chat, and showing off her trademark smile, she asked how long until my sister was arriving, before falling peacefully into her slumber.

After about half an hour or so, Mum's doctor popped her head in for her daily visit to check on, not only Mum, but all of her other patients as well. Mum woke up for a short time with the doctor asking, 'Tired, Julie?' to which Mum nodded and mumbled, 'Yes'. It was after this moment that I excused myself from the room to go to the bathroom.

After excusing myself and completing a quick coffee run, I walked back to Mum's room, passing her doctor in the hallway with a stern, concerned look on her face. Once I got back into Mum's room, I was told that they were upping her medication and they weren't giving her long.

Fuck.

We'd previously had these open conversations about death and knowing when it was your time, but to actually hear that she didn't have long was like a dagger through the heart time and time again. And then when you think you can't possibly take anymore, the dagger was inserted a number of times more.

Now, up until this point Mum had been sharing a room in palliative care, and as I began contacting all our family members to make their way to the hospital to say their goodbyes, the doctors were frantically organising Mum to be moved to a room on her own.

By lunchtime that afternoon, Mum was moved to her own room and family members began arriving. Time was split between the family room, the courtyard garden and checking in on Mum. But as the day grew old and tired, sadly, so did Mum. Her breathing began to slow, and her body grew weary.

On April 23rd, my mum Julie Smith passed away peacefully surrounded by all her loved ones.

And after fighting for what was almost nine years to the month, her body could no longer sustain fighting the good fight. As you can imagine, emotional scenes followed the night. I just remember crying uncontrollably. I cried so much my chest actually began to hurt. Maybe I was finally letting out everything I had held in from the past 12 months since Mum's initial decline?

If calling family members a couple of weeks earlier was the first thing I thought I could never see myself doing, then to say I would be removing Mum's piercings from her as she lay resting peacefully was definitely another.

The only thing I could do as I sobbed was to apologise time and time again while removing her piercings and jewellery. After removing her piercings and jewellery, I gave Mum one final kiss to her forehead, and left the room.

As I left the room, one of the nurses carefully closed Mum's door. As I walked away, I remember turning around to see the closed door with a beautiful butterfly poster on it. And I thought it was quite fitting that there was a butterfly on the door. For me, it seemed like from the moment Mum was first admitted into hospital a couple of weeks earlier, she was in a cocoon, but from the moment she took her last breath, she had become a beautiful butterfly, and she was finally free to fly away.

Arriving home that night and seeing our dog Rosie excited to see us and not understanding what was going on, added another dimension of hurt that we didn't need. After a couple of shots of a horrible and strong- alcoholic drink, I made my way to bed to sleep. How much sleep? I wasn't quite sure.

Lying there, staring at the ceiling, I was expecting someone to come out of nowhere and say, 'Sorry, this is an absolute cruel joke, your mother is actually fine and she will be home with you all soon enough.' But sadly, it was reality, and although we didn't want to believe it, we knew what lay ahead would surely allow the inevitable to truly sink in.

The following few days were a blur. There were visitors and flowers arriving one after the other. I remember watching movies with Mum when I was younger, and seeing grieving families receiving endless amounts of flowers and thinking, 'Wow, a person who receives that many flowers must have had a lot of friends,' and this is definitely true of Mum.

Anzac Day was a couple of days later, and as hard as it was, I made my way to watch my footy team play against another local footy team. I was meant to play, but seeing how quickly Mum's health had deteriorated, I pulled out of the match earlier on in the day of April 23rd. After a solid afternoon, the boys dominated the game to a win. Upon leaving the ground that night,

Dad and I knew reality would set in the following day as we would be heading to the funeral directors to sort out details of the funeral and the wake to follow.

The 10 days between Mum's passing and Mum's funeral were an absolute blur. Looking back now, I just remember feeling numb, but there was also a sense of urgency. Dad and I had visited the funeral directors and organised Mum's funeral, as well as organising her wake. Dad and I stopped for a coffee on the way home and we sat across from each other in silence.

I just kept thinking that no one should have to go through this and be planning a funeral. And for Dad, I know he was thinking that he shouldn't have been planning his younger wife's funeral.

That afternoon, I had a chiropractic appointment. The last time I had seen him was just before Mum was first admitted to hospital. Interestingly enough, he also used to look after my mum when she was having trouble with her back. So while I was laying there, he asked me, 'How is your Mum doing?' I could feel the tears about to start when I lifted my head and told him that she had passed away three days ago. While he was understandably upset, his thoughts immediately went to seeing how my Dad, sister and I were coping. And all I said was that for the moment, I was hanging in there.

I think the hardest thing I realised during that 10 day period was that while most of our family and friends continued on with their lives, and made their way back to work, our lives sort of stopped for that period.

On 1 May, 2019, I celebrated my 28th birthday, the first without Mum. Although Mum made us feel special every other day of the year, she always went that little bit extra on our birthdays. From when I was a little kid, Mum would always make our favourite meal for our birthday. For me, the meal I had the most on my birthdays was an egg and bacon pie, and in most recent years, homemade pasties. The hardest thing to come to grips with was not receiving any handwritten birthday cards anymore, but also that I would never have her egg and bacon pies anymore. Thankfully, my Nan had made the pie for me. Although it wasn't the best birthday I have had, I can honestly say that there was a lot of love in that room, and I know Mum would be looking down with her trademark smile.

Well, it was the night before Mum's funeral, her final goodbye. I couldn't fucking sleep because I knew that after we said our final goodbyes tomorrow, that would be it. We would begin to grieve and slowly move on with our lives. It seemed unfair. Unfair, because there are people in the world who take their lives for granted, and continue to live long (often troubled lives), yet some people, in this case my mum, who always looked after herself and strived to live a healthy life, had her life cut short. As my thoughts grew weary, I fell into a gradual sleep, knowing tomorrow would be probably the most difficult day in my 28 years.

Two days on from my birthday, on May 3rd, we farewelled her with a rockstar reception with well over 200 people attending the ceremony and over 100 joining us at the wake to further celebrate her life. As far as funerals and wakes go, the day overall would be just how Mum would have wanted it. The sun was out with hardly a cloud in sight, which was kind of reminiscent of Mum throughout her lifetime. When moments seemed dark, she was always the sun, providing warmth and light to break through the darkness.

It was amazing to see that in her 54 years, Mum had affected so many lives in a positive way and that everyone was there to celebrate her life.

One of those lives was a friend of mine, Jemma. Jemma, sadly, was also battling breast cancer, which had eventually spread to various parts of her body as well. She fought it for as long as she could, but sadly at the age of 26, Jemma joined Mum at the golden gates in the sky, almost two months on from Mum's funeral. And as hard as it was, and as sick and tired as she was at the time, she willed herself out of bed and made sure she could attend Mum's funeral. Both Mum and Jemma often chatted to each other about their experiences and as Mum had been through chemotherapy and radiation well before Jemma had been diagnosed, Jemma would often seek advice from Mum about what to expect. For the most part, Mum always left out the 'nitty-gritty' details because she didn't want to scare her, or have her worry, but little did she know that Jemma was stronger than she or anyone else could have thought. I suppose the only thing that can bring both families closure is that they are both up there, sharing battle stories and looking after one another.

For most people, Mum was a daughter, sister, niece, aunt, close friend, a best friend and a work colleague. But simply, for my sister and me, she was our mum, and for my dad, his number one girl in the world.

As the sun set on that day, we slowly made our way home. Our hearts were heavy with the final goodbyes to Mum, but we were thankful we could all share our memories with all of our friends and family.

Firsts

We knew losing a loved one would never get easier, and shortly after Mum's funeral someone mentioned that the year of 'firsts' would be the hardest. And that once you get through the first birthday, the first Mother's Day, the first wedding anniversary, it will begin to get easier, and sadly, we experienced a lot of firsts in the space of a month after Mum passed away. My first birthday without her around was tough, and still seeing her name on my birthday card broke me. A couple weeks after my birthday, it was Mum and Dad's 30th wedding anniversary, a day he particularly struggled through as he did a couple of days later on his 73rd birthday.

Since Mum has been gone, I feel like a little bit of all of us died along with her. Dad has definitely lost that spark that he once had, and the little twinkle in his eye. I'm definitely not the same person I was a year ago. Do I wish I was the happy-go-lucky guy I was then? Yes and no. I'm doing the best I can at the moment, but my perspective on life and everything I wanted has definitely changed.

Throughout Mum's battle, and more specifically from her rapid decline in August 2018, Mum always reminded us that if we ever needed help to deal with grief or any mental health issues, a grief counsellor or psychologist would be the way to go. And although I considered it while Mum was alive, I held off because I was telling myself that I had to be strong in front of her and for her, because if I fell apart how would she find the strength to carry on?

But finally, while I was still off from work and dealing with the loss of Mum, I made my way to my local GP to have a Mental Health Plan organised. While it was hard to admit that I needed help, looking back now I can say that it was the best thing I could have done. I found myself having feelings of being useless and not deserving love or to be loved. I felt that even though I tried to do everything I could to help Mum while she was at home, I ultimately couldn't save her, and I think that it took me some time to understand.

There have been a lot of times since Mum's passing that family, friends and people in general have asked how I'm coping. And what I have said to them is probably way worse than saying the way I was actually feeling. I said I was fine and I was doing okay, when in retrospect I should have said, 'You know what? I'm

fucking struggling, and I'm not fine. I'm not alright.'
Why didn't I tell them that? I'm not quite sure. Maybe
my loved ones were dealing with their own troubles and
I wanted to ease their stress by not adding my grief
and struggles onto what they were dealing with? To
those who asked and continue to ask how I am, I thank
you. And to those who thought I was alright because I
was too ashamed to say that I wasn't, I am sorry.

But thankfully, after many sessions with my psychologist
I was able to see things more clearly, and I was able
to process everything I was experiencing. I see now
that no matter what I did while Mum was alive, at the
end of the day I couldn't control whether she lived or
didn't. And as much as I wish I had that ability, the way
I helped her is something she would always remember,
and something I should constantly remind myself of
as being a positive and happy memory with Mum while
she was alive.

I encourage anyone who is feeling down or doesn't
think they are in the best shape, mentally (even if you
can't speak to a GP straight away) to tell a friend or
family member how they are feeling so that together
you can work toward taking positive steps in looking
after your mental health.

And don't be afraid to let people in. I think in the end I
found it hard to let people in, even those closest to me,
because I felt like there was a cloud over me. Normally I

would make clear and rational decisions, but it was like my mind was an old Windows 97 PC and I just couldn't get it working properly, which was both frustrating and disheartening. I felt like I couldn't explain my thoughts to anyone because it didn't make sense to me. Had I not asked for help, even though some important personal relationships have since been strained, I feel things could have been a lot worse had I not taken the step.

From One Mother to Another

The irony of writing this book dedicated to my Mum is that she was an absolute lover of books. An avid reader. I always said that she was at her happiest when watching her favourite TV shows snuggled up in her pyjamas by 2pm on a cold winter's afternoon, or when she was sitting by herself, indoors and out, with a warm cup of tea and a good book. Romance, crime, thriller, regardless what type of novel, she would always immerse herself in a book so much so that she could rattle off information about the characters like she had been friends with them for 30 years.

I feel like Mum gained her love of books from her mother, my Nan, Jacqueline. She would always say she was reading books to Mum, even at a young age. And while my Nan was often reading books on other events to my mum, I thought it would be good for a change to have others read the events that shaped Mum into who she was.

That's why I asked her mum, my Nan, to write a little passage on her thoughts throughout Mum's battle. And while it had taken her many times and a fair few tears to write what she thought perfectly encapsulated Mum's battle, this is what she had to say:

As a mum to Julie, her diagnosis of having breast cancer was hard to accept, as it was for her as well. I shed many tears, but quickly realised I needed to be positive for Jules' sake, as throughout her lifetime she was a very positive person.

She went through chemotherapy, radiation and countless operations like a champ. She had her good days and her not so good days. As her cancer reappeared elsewhere in her body, the same routine applied.

During recovery, she was able to get away to different places for a break. We shared tears at times, then picked ourselves up and 'got on with it'. During each battle, she had many visitors

– family, siblings and her friends. They came armed with flowers, gifts, food galore, love, laughter and just their presence.

At times, Julie would say, 'Okay guys, it's quiet time now'. We knew then she was either ready for bed, looking to use her phone or just resting her eyes. She would say to me, 'Sshh, now Mum'. I'd get up and go to leave and she would say, 'Don't go, stay there'. I was happy to oblige.

Jool, you had a good childhood, did all of your schooling well as well as TAFE. You chose childcare which you worked at for years. You had many friends and many good times.

You met and married Ron and had Dylan and Emily, and you were a great mother to them, too. You were always so very proud of them.

When Dylan and Emily were both at school, you often helped out in their classrooms. It was later that you began working as a canteen assistant. A fair few years later, you then applied for a teacher's aide position, for which you were accepted. You loved the job and made many friends, many of whom visited you often to see how you were going.

Jool, I'm very glad we had that chat out in the garden at the hospital. I will always remember that. You wanted us to be present when you passed away and we were. It was the hardest thing I have ever endured.

Jool, thank you for being a lovely, caring and gentle daughter. We were so very proud of you. Memories we will treasure forever.

Love Mum + Dad.

P.S. Dylan, thank you for asking me to write this chapter.

– Love Nan

Don't You Forget About Me

I thought of many names to call this book. But nothing seemed to do Mum any sort of justice. I wanted something that would immediately make anyone who read this and knew her say, 'Yes that was Julie, alright'. I was quickly set on the name Jewel. I feel the name best represents her as a person, as her nickname was Jool or Jules. But for anyone who had met her, she was definitely a jewel in our family, and on occasion if you caught her in the right light she would sparkle and light up the room.

Mum was always a big advocate for being open and honest, and even though I said all I wanted to say to her, I feel it is only fitting that she deserve a *This is Your Life* styled ending to truly celebrate her life.

I have written and re-written many ways to describe my Mum and detail her journey with cancer. My sister

Emily said it best at her funeral that cancer didn't win. Mum won. In my head, I often described cancer arriving like a thief in the night and stealing my old mum away from me. And just when we thought we caught the little bastard, and it would leave us alone, it would return again disguised in different parts of her body and come back to steal more of the mum I knew away from me.

But Mum, after almost nine years of fighting, from being left barely able to stand or walk after treatments, to days where the only solace you had was to stay in bed because any upright movements caused you to be dizzy and nauseous, you are finally at peace now. Your smile remained throughout all of your treatments and your tough days. I guess looking back now, I can see how bad those days were for you, but at the time, I thought to myself *'Wow, if she's still smiling even while dealing with cancer, it mustn't be that bad'*. I was so wrong and so naive.

I will always remember the day we both went for our learner's permit together. We both passed, but because you scored 97 percent and I scored 94 percent, you always held that over me even in your final days. Mum, I was so happy that I could share a half completed rough draft of this book with you. You laughed when I was younger and I said, 'Maybe I'll write a book one day'. I wasn't too bad in school when it came to English class, but I never really had the motivation to take it seriously.

And had you told me then that one day I would write a book, I would have been the one laughing. But looking back, I definitely had a motivation to write what I thought and felt, and Mum, that motivation was you. I hope this book sparks pride and joy and that my love for you shines through in every page. This book is not only dedicated to you, but to everyone who has fought cancer and to those who are still fighting some sort of cancer. Keep fighting!

One thing Mum prided herself on was her memory, and how reliable she was at recalling information (and boy, could we use that memory right now while looking for things around the house) and I am so thankful that now, her memory will live on in this book.

Until I see you again, Mum, I hope I can keep making you proud.

Now, I was hoping to be able to sign this off on some sort of Judd Nelson moment with my fist thrust into the air as *Don't You (Forget About Me)* played in the background, but unfortunately the universe works in mysterious ways, and in this case it continues to work against us. You would think after all we had endured with Mum we were due for our luck to change, but unfortunately this isn't the case, and our dance with the devil known as cancer (and that other 'C' word that we can't say) has begun again.

In August 2019, after initially not feeling like himself and having multiple scans, Dad has unfortunately found out that he has stage 4 melanoma in his liver and lungs, and he is riddled with melanoma growths, predominantly on his bones. Within a week of that diagnosis, Dad began immunotherapy treatment, with radiation soon to follow. If the treatment doesn't work, or Dad chooses to stop treatment, they are more than likely giving him a couple of months, but we are hoping for the treatment to control his cancer growths, so Dad can see the next couple of years through.

But if any little bit of Mum has remained with Dad, I really hope it's the strength to fight for as long and as hard as she did. I know she is up there waiting for him to come home to her, but she will have to wait patiently until his time has come.

'There is no place like home.'

Judy Garland, The Wizard of Oz, 1939

www.ingramcontent.com/pod-product-compliance
Lightning Source LLC
Chambersburg PA
CBHW021122080526
44587CB00010B/606